AIR and WATER EXPERIMENTS

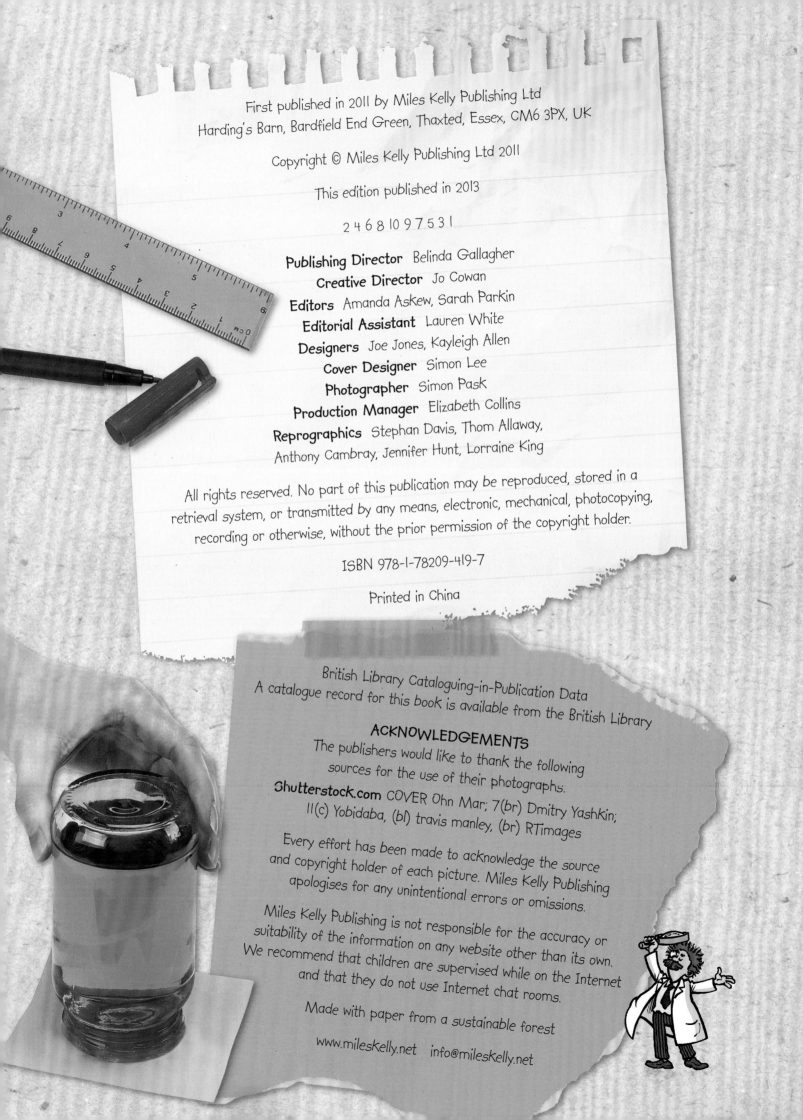

First published in 2011 by Miles Kelly Publishing Ltd
Harding's Barn, Bardfield End Green, Thaxted, Essex, CM6 3PX, UK

This edition published in 2013

2 4 6 8 10 9 7 5 3 1

Publishing Director Belinda Gallagher
Creative Director Jo Cowan
Editors Amanda Askew, Sarah Parkin
Editorial Assistant Lauren White
Designers Joe Jones, Kayleigh Allen
Cover Designer Simon Lee
Photographer Simon Pask
Production Manager Elizabeth Collins
Reprographics Stephan Davis, Thom Allaway,
Anthony Cambray, Jennifer Hunt, Lorraine King

ISBN 978-1-78209-419-7

Printed in China

British Library Cataloguing-in-Publication Data
A catalogue record for this book is available from the British Library

ACKNOWLEDGEMENTS
The publishers would like to thank the following
sources for the use of their photographs:
Shutterstock.com COVER Ohn Mar; 7(br) Dmitry Yashkin;
11(c) Yobidaba, (bl) travis manley, (br) RTimages

Every effort has been made to acknowledge the source
and copyright holder of each picture. Miles Kelly Publishing
apologises for any unintentional errors or omissions.

Made with paper from a sustainable forest

www.mileskelly.net   info@mileskelly.net

SUPER SCIENCE

AIR and WATER EXPERIMENTS

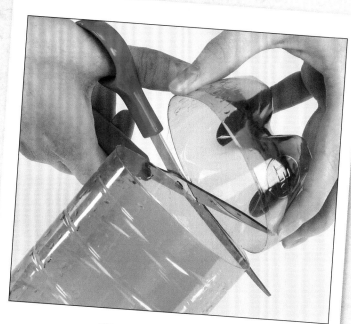

Chris Oxlade
Consultant: John Farndon

Miles Kelly

CONTENTS

Learn all about air and water, including how air pressure works and what materials float.

Do candles need oxygen to burn? Find out on page 28.

Experiment time!

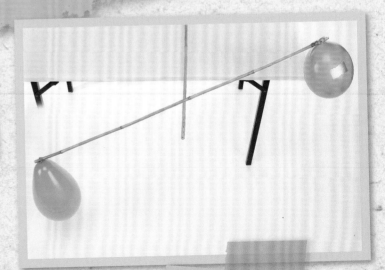

Why do boats float? Find out on page 13.

Does air have weight? Find out on page 19.

Notes for HELPERS

Help needed

Help and hazards

- All of the experiments are suitable for children to conduct, but they will need help and supervision with some. This is usually because the experiment requires the use of matches to light candles, a knife or scissors for cutting, or food colouring. These experiments are marked with a 'Help needed' symbol.

- Read the instructions together before starting and help to assemble the equipment before supervising the experiment.

- It may be useful to carry out your own risk assessment to avoid any possible hazards before your child begins. Check that long hair and any loose clothing are tied back.

- Check that materials such as matches and scissors are put away safely after use.

Also try...

Extra experiments

You can also help your children with the extra experiments in this book, or search the Internet for more, similar ideas. There are hundreds of science experiment websites to choose from.

www.kids-science-experiments.com This website is packed with simple, fun experiments for your children to enjoy.

www.sciencebob.com/experiments/index.php Engaging science experiments with clearly explained instructions will keep your kids busy for hours.

www.tryscience.org You will find lots of entertaining and informative experiments on this colourful, interactive website.

All about AIR!

You can't see it, but you can't live without it! Air is all around us, and it contains the oxygen we need in order to live. Air has weight, and it is pressing on you all the time, although you won't be aware of it.

Air pressure

Tiny particles in air, called molecules, are always bumping into each other. The more this happens, the greater the air pressure. The higher up you go, the lower the air pressure, and the less oxygen there is in the air.

In the air

The air consists of a mixture of gases, mainly nitrogen and oxygen, and also dust and moisture.

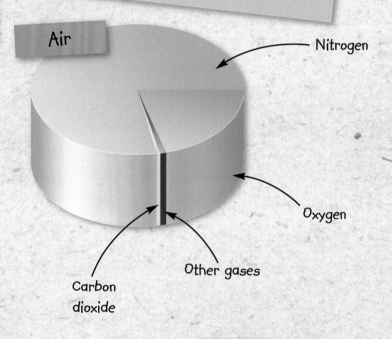

Air

Nitrogen

Oxygen

Other gases

Carbon dioxide

Atmosphere

Exosphere
500–800 km

Thermosphere
80–500 km

Mesosphere
50–80 km

Stratosphere
10–50 km

Troposphere
0–10 km

The atmosphere

Our planet is wrapped up in a blanket of air. We call this blanket of many layers the atmosphere. It stretches hundreds of kilometres above our heads. The atmosphere keeps in heat at night, and protects us from the Sun's rays during the day.

All about WATER!

All life depends on water – no animals or plants could survive without it. Most of the world's water is in the oceans and is salty. Fresh water, with no salt, is found in rivers and lakes.

Three forms of water

Water is the only substance that can exist as a solid (ice), a liquid (water) and a gas (steam) at normal temperatures. It melts at 0°C and boils at 100°C.

Water molecules

Water is made of two hydrogen atoms and one oxygen atom. It has a chemical formula of H_2O. A water molecule is shaped like the letter 'V'.

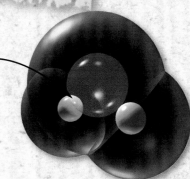

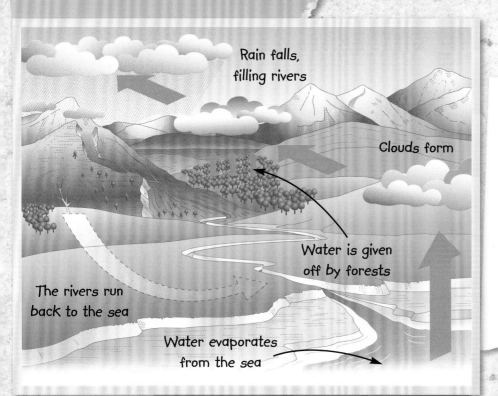

Rain falls, filling rivers

Clouds form

Water is given off by forests

The rivers run back to the sea

Water evaporates from the sea

The water cycle

All the water on Earth is involved in the water cycle. Water droplets or vapours rise from lakes, rivers and seas to form clouds. These droplets join to make bigger drops that eventually fall as rain. Much of the rain runs back into the sea.

Floating and sinking

When an object is placed in liquid, its weight displaces (pushes away) a volume of the liquid. This liquid pushes back on the solid with a force called 'upthrust'. If the upthrust is equal to or greater than the object's weight, the solid will float. An object will sink until its weight is equal to the upthrust of the water.

Using this book

Each experiment has numbered instructions and clear explanations about your findings. Read through all the instructions before you start an experiment, and then follow them carefully, one at a time. If you are not sure what to do, ask an adult.

Experiment symbols

① Shows how long the experiment will take once you have collected all the equipment you need.

② Shows if you need to ask an adult to help you with the experiment.

③ Shows how easy or difficult the experiment is to do.

Introduction
See what you will be learning about in each experiment.

Things you will need
You should be able to find the equipment around the house or from a supermarket. No special equipment is needed. Always ask before using materials from home.

⚠️ Safety
If there is a 'Help needed' symbol at the start of the experiment, you must ask an adult to help you.

The warning symbol also tells you to be careful when using knives or scissors, or matches. Always ask an adult for help.

The magic of AIR

Air is all around us and it also presses on us – with a push called air pressure. Get ready to see the amazing power of air pressure.

① 30 min ② No help needed ③ Hard

You will need
- work surface
- 2 clean, empty jars
- washing-up bowl
- petroleum jelly
- square of thin card (bigger than the jar opening)
- optional: food colouring

1a Fill a jar with water (make it coloured for fun). Smear the rim of the jar with a thick layer of petroleum jelly.

Hold the jar over a washing-up bowl, just in case

1c Support the card with one hand and turn the over. Take your hand away from the card.

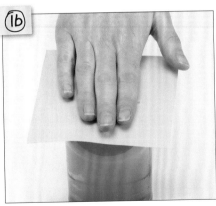

1b Put a square of card on the jar, so that it touches the rim all round.

Q Can card hold water?

A Yes, air pressure pushing up on the card keeps the water in the glass. This shows that air pressure pushes in all directions, not just down.

22

Labels
Handy labels will provide you with useful tips and information to help your experiment run smoothly.

Stages
Numbers and letters guide you through the stages of each experiment.

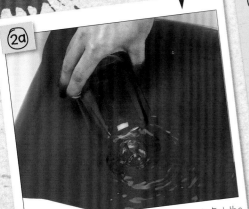

(2a)

Fill a bowl with coloured water (just for fun). Put the jar underwater so that it fills with water. Then stand the jar up so that the opening is underneath.

(2b)

Slowly lift the jar upwards out of the water. To begin with, the opening is underwater – what happens as you lift the jar more?

Q Does the water stay in?
A Yes, the water inside the jar should stay where it is instead of spilling out. It only spills out when the rim of the glass leaves the water. Air pressure pushes down on the water's surface. This pressure pushes the water up inside the jar.

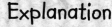

Explanation
At the end of each experiment is a question-and-answer explanation. It tells you what should have happened and why.

Whoosh!

Also try...
Pour warm water into a plastic drinks bottle until the bottle is about a third full. Swirl the water around the bottle a few times and pour it away. Put the top on the bottle and plunge it into cold water. The warm water he~ inside the bottle. When you put the b~ water, the air inside contracts, which ~ air pressure inside the bottle, and t~ air pressure outside squashes the ~

Also try...
Simple mini experiments to test the science you've learnt.

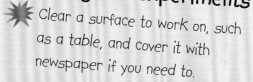
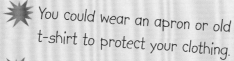

Doing the experiments

✹ Clear a surface to work on, such as a table, and cover it with newspaper if you need to.

✹ You could wear an apron or old t-shirt to protect your clothing.

✹ Gather all the equipment you need before you start, and tidy up after each experiment.

✹ Ask an adult to help you when an experiment is marked with a 'Help needed' or warning symbol.

✹ Work over a tray or sink when you are pouring water.

✹ Always ask an adult to help if you are unsure what to do.

Scientist KIT

Before you begin experimenting, you will need to gather some equipment. You should be able to find all of it around the house or from a local supermarket. Ask an adult's permission before using anything and take care when you see a warning sign.

Foody things

• food colouring
• milk
• sandwich bag

Handy hint!
Milk should be kept in the fridge. When you have taken the amount you need for your experiment, put it back in the fridge or it will go off.

Milk

Food colouring

Paper clips

Straw

From the kitchen

• glass
• jars
• jug
• large plastic drinks bottles
• plate
• scissors
• shallow bowl
• small bowl
• small plate
• straws
• washing-up bowl
• washing-up liquid
• water

From the craft box

• card tube
• craft knife
• marker pen
• modelling clay or sticky tack
• paper clips
• pin
• ruler
• stapler
• sticky tape
• string
• tape measure
• thick card
• thin card
• tissue paper

Sticky tack

Scissors

Thin card

Card tube

 Warning!
Scissors and Knives are extremely sharp and can cut you easily. Make sure you ask an adult for help. When passing scissors or a Knife, always point the blunt end towards the other person.

Handy hint!
Next time you finish a Kitchen or toilet roll, keep hold of the cardboard tube found inside. It will be useful for experiments.

Balloons

Handy hint!
In some of the experiments, you can use food colouring, but it is not essential. However, it will make the experiment clearer and you can choose any colour you like!

Other stuff
- balloons
- 2 chairs
- coins
- cotton buds
- duct tape
- hair dryer
- long cane, about 1.5 m
- matches
- petroleum jelly
- shorter cane, about 1 m
- small block of wood
- small candle

Hair dryer

Cotton buds

⚠ Warning!
When using matches or candles, ask an adult for help. Fire is very dangerous, so you must be very careful around it.

⚠ Warning!
Electricity and water do not mix and will cause an electric shock. When using a hair dryer, make sure that there is no water around you.

Places you'll need to work
- large space
- work surface

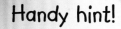

♻ Remember to recycle and re-use
One way to help the environment is by recycling and re-using materials such as glass, paper, plastics and scrap metals. It is mostly cheaper and less wasteful than making new products from stratch.

Re-using means you use materials again in their original form rather than throwing them away.

Recycling is when materials are taken to a plant where they can be melted and re-made into either the same or new products.

Handy hint!
Plastic bottles come in many different colours. Try to use a clear bottle so that you can see your experiment working.

FLOAT or sink

In these experiments, you see that some things float and some things sink. You can also see why materials that normally sink can be used to make boats that float.

You will need

- work surface
- washing-up bowl or sink
- balloon
- water
- small block of wood
- small bowl
- small plate
- modelling clay or sticky tack
- optional: food colouring

1

Push down

Fill the washing-up bowl with water. Blow up the balloon and tie a knot in it. Put the balloon in the water and push it under. Then let go.

Q Does the balloon float?

A Yes, when you push the balloon underwater and let go, the water pushes the balloon back up. This is called the buoyant force. Water always pushes up on anything you put in it. The size of the force on an object depends on how much water the object pushes out of the way.

2

Put the piece of wood in the bowl of water. Push it underwater and then let go.

Q Does the wood float?

A Yes, the wood floats. When it is underwater, the buoyant force on the wood is larger than its weight, so it floats to the surface.

③

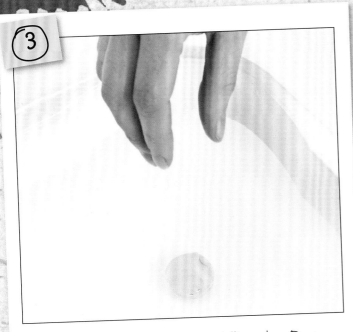

Roll a ball of sticky tack or modelling clay. Drop this in the water, too.

⒬ Does clay sink?

Ⓐ **Yes, it sinks.** This happens because the buoyant force on the ball of clay is less than its weight.

④a

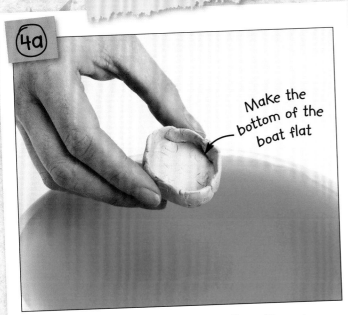

Make the bottom of the boat flat

Put a small bowl on a plate and fill it with water, right to the top. You could add food colouring so you can see the results clearly. Mould a piece of modelling clay into a boat shape and carefully lower it into the water.

④b

Make some small balls of modelling clay as cargo for your boat. Add them one at a time to the boat.

⒬ Does it sink?

Ⓐ **Yes, eventually it will sink.** At first, when you make the clay into a boat, its shape means that it pushes aside much more water than before, so it floats. As you load it up with cargo, it sinks down, so the buoyant force gets larger, balancing the extra weight. You can see that more water is pushed aside as some water overflows the top of the bowl!

Sunk!

Water overboard

FUN
fountains

Turn on the tap and water pours out. But it doesn't come out by itself – it gets pushed. The push is water pressure in the pipe. Here's an experiment that shows water pressure at work.

15 min | Help needed | Easy

You will need

- work surface
- large plastic drinks bottle
- craft knife
- ruler
- water
- jug
- marker pen
- washing-up bowl
- optional: food colouring

1a

10 cm from the bottom of the bottle

Remove the lid of a large plastic drinks bottle and draw a mark about 10 cm above the base. Using a craft knife, carefully cut a neat, round hole about 5 mm across. Ask an adult to help you.

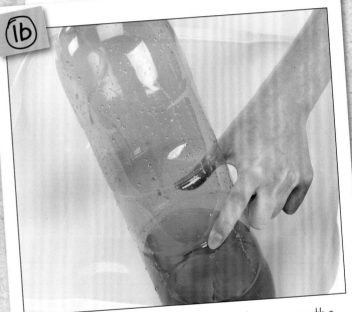

1b

Fill a jug with coloured water (to help you see the water later). Stand the bottle in a washing-up bowl. Put your finger over the hole and fill the bottle to the top with the water. Then quickly take your finger away.

Whoosh!

Q What happens to the water?

A The water shoots from the bottle. It is pushed out by the water pressure, which is caused by the weight of the water above the hole.

2a

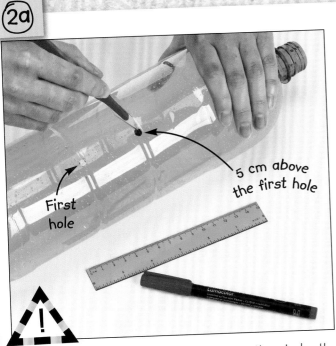

First hole

5 cm above the first hole

Carefully empty the bottle and cut another hole, the same size as the first, 5 cm above the first hole.

2b

Refill the bottle, again keeping your fingers over the holes to stop the water leaking out. Release both fingers at the same time.

Ⓠ What happens?

Ⓐ The bottom fountain is longer at first and then it quickly becomes shorter.

The pressure is made by the weight of the water pressing down from above the level of each hole. In deep water, the pressure is higher. The lower hole is deeper in the water, so the pressure is higher, making the fountain longer. As the water runs out of the holes, the water level falls, so the weight of the water above the holes reduces. The pressure at the holes drops, so the fountains gradually get shorter.

Going...

going...

gone!

SKINNY water

You use water every day, but did you know that it has a skin? Here are some experiments to investigate how this skin works.

You will need

- work surface
- shallow bowl
- paper clips
- water
- square of tissue paper (smaller than the bowl)
- washing-up liquid
- cotton buds
- clean, empty jar
- coins
- plate
- milk
- food colouring

1a

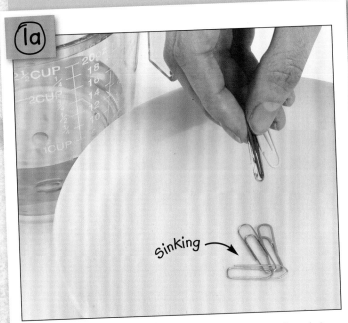

sinking →

Fill a bowl with water. Drop some paper clips into the water from just above the surface.

1b

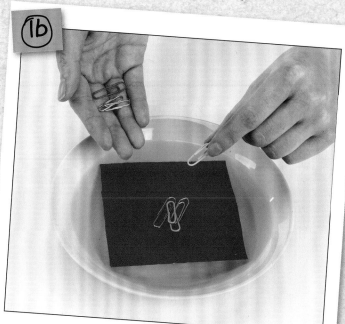

Carefully place the tissue paper onto the water's surface. Now place a few paper clips onto it.

1c

Put some of washing-up liquid on the cotton bud

Put some washing-up liquid on a cotton bud and touch the water's surface.

Ⓠ Do paper clips float?

Ⓐ **No!** They are made of steel, which is heavier than water, so they sink. However, the surface of water can stop them from sinking because it acts like a skin. This is called surface tension where the water molecules at the surface are pulled towards each other. The tissue paper helps you to put the clips gently into the water so that surface tension can support them. Washing-up liquid breaks the surface tension, so the paper clips sink.

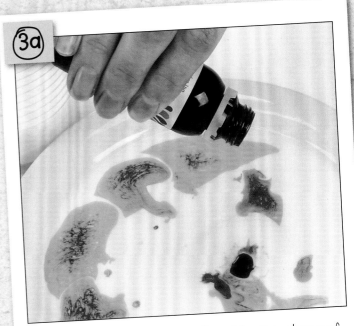

Fill a plate with milk. Carefully add a few drops of food colouring to the milk to make coloured spots.

(2)

Put a plate underneath to catch spills

Fill a jar to the brim with coloured water (so you can *see* what's happening). Gently drop coins, one by one, into the water and watch what happens.

(3b)

Dip a cotton bud into some washing-up liquid and touch the surface of the milk. What happens?

Q Does water bulge?

A Yes, the water surface gets gradually higher – until it is higher than the rim of the jar. Surface tension stops water overflowing from the top of the jar as you drop coins in.

Q What does washing-up liquid do to the food colouring?

A It breaks surface tension in some places. Then the surface tension in other places pulls the food colouring into patterns.

Bulge!

Pretty patterns

Balloon SEESAW

Air is all around us, both indoors and outdoors. You can't feel it pressing down, so it's easy to think that it doesn't weigh anything. Try this experiment to show that it does.

 15 min

 Help needed

 Tricky

You will need

- large space
- flat work surface
- long cane, about 1.5 m
- shorter cane, about 1 m
- 2 balloons
- duct tape
- sticky tape
- pin

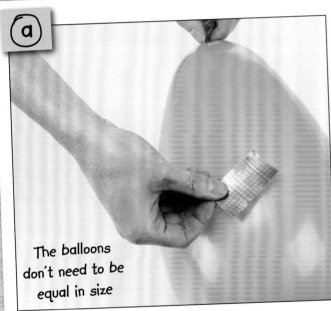

(a)

The balloons don't need to be equal in size

Blow up two balloons and tie their necks. Don't put in too much air or they will burst later. Cut a piece of duct tape about 5 cm long and stick it to one balloon.

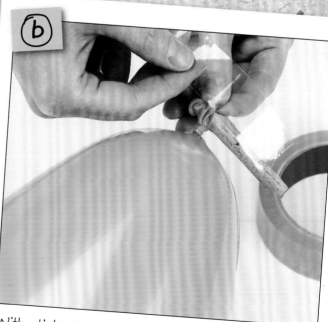

(b)

With sticky tape, attach the necks of the balloons to either end of the longer cane. The balloons should stick out at right angles, and both be on the same side of the cane.

Fix the shorter cane to a flat work surface so it doesn't move, with at least 50 cm of it hanging over the edge. You could use sticky tape or heavy books. This cane will support the long cane.

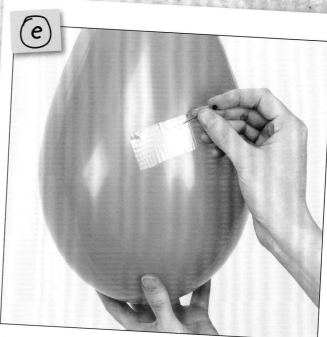

Carefully push a pin through the centre of the duct tape on the balloon to make a small hole. This will let air leak out slowly.

d

Have patience!
This is tricky

Rest the centre of the long cane on the short cane. Carefully move the long cane left and right, bit by bit, until it is balanced.

Q What happens as the balloon goes down?

A When you blow up the balloons, you squeeze air into them to stretch the elastic. So each balloon is full of squashed air. With the cane perfectly balanced, there is the same weight on each side of the balance point. When you prick the balloon, air begins to escape. Very slowly, this balloon begins to rise and the other begins to fall. This means weight is being lost from the balloon. So the escaping air must have weight.

Wheeeee!...

ROCKET balloons

When air rushes out of a balloon, the balloon flies off. How far it flies partly depends on how much air comes out. Get ready for take off!

15 min   No help needed   Easy

You will need

- large space
- 2 chairs
- 2 long balloons
- 2 straws
- string
- sticky tape
- paper clips
- tape measure

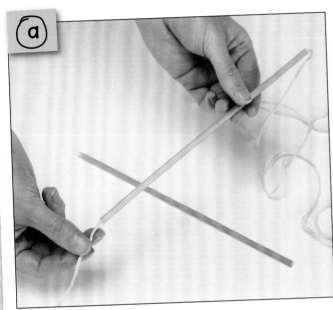

(a) Cut two lengths of string, each about 5 metres long. Thread a straw onto each piece of string.

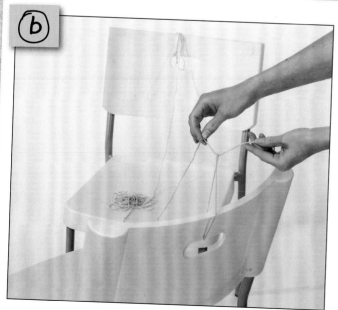

(b) Tie or stick the string to the two chairs and pull the chairs apart so the string is taut. You'll need a large space to do this.

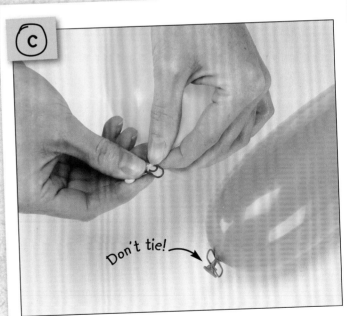

(c) Don't tie!

Blow up one balloon completely, and the other balloon only half full of air. Twist the ends and attach a paper clip to stop the air from escaping.

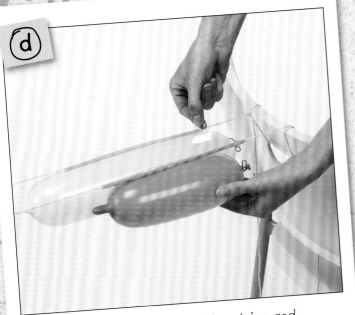

(d) Pull the straws to one end of the string and attach the balloons using sticky tape.

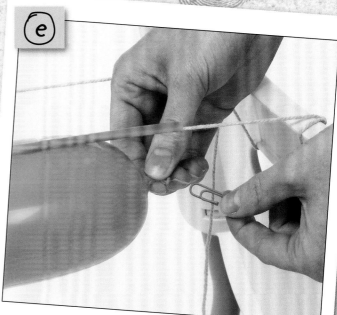

(e) Carefully remove each paper clip. Make sure the neck of each balloon isn't sticking together. Let the balloons go and watch how far they travel.

Whoooooooooooooosh! You can't catch me!

Q Which balloon travels the furthest?

A The balloon with the most air inside. The air inside a balloon is under pressure because the balloon is trying to squash it. When you remove the paper clips, the pressure pushes the air out. As the air comes out in one direction, it pushes the balloon in the opposite direction, just like a rocket. More air comes out of the bigger balloon, and at first is comes out faster. So the bigger balloon goes further.

The magic of AIR

Air is all around us and it also presses on us – with a push called air pressure. Get ready to see the amazing power of air pressure.

 30 min   No help needed   Hard

You will need

- work surface
- 2 clean, empty jars
- washing-up bowl
- petroleum jelly
- square of thin card (bigger than the jar opening)
- optional: food colouring

1a Fill a jar with water (make it coloured for fun). Smear the rim of the jar with a thick layer of petroleum jelly.

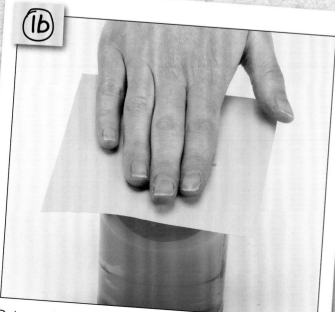

1b Put a square of card on the jar, so that it touches the rim all round.

1c Hold the jar over a washing-up bowl, just in case

Support the card with one hand and turn the jar over. Take your hand away from the card.

Q Can card hold water?

A Yes, air pressure pushing up on the card keeps the water in the glass. This shows that air pressure pushes in all directions, not just down.

2a

Fill a bowl with coloured water (just for fun). Put the jar underwater so that it fills with water. Then stand the jar up so that the opening is underneath.

2b

Slowly lift the jar upwards out of the water. To begin with, the opening is underwater – what happens as you lift the jar more?

Also try...

Pour warm water into a plastic drinks bottle until the bottle is about a third full. Swirl the water around the bottle a few times and pour it away. Put the top on the bottle and plunge it into cold water. The warm water heats the air inside the bottle. When you put the bottle in cold water, the air inside contracts, which reduces the air pressure inside the bottle, and the higher air pressure outside squashes the bottle.

Q Does the water stay in?

A Yes, the water inside the jar should stay where it is instead of spilling out. It only spills out when the rim of the glass leaves the water. Air pressure pushes down on the water's surface. This pressure pushes the water up inside the jar.

Whoosh!

Blowing TRICKS

This experiment demonstrates another property of air pressure – when air moves faster, its pressure goes down.

15 min Help needed Easy

You will need

- work surface
- small balloon
- large plastic drinks bottle
- card tube
- sandwich bag
- scissors

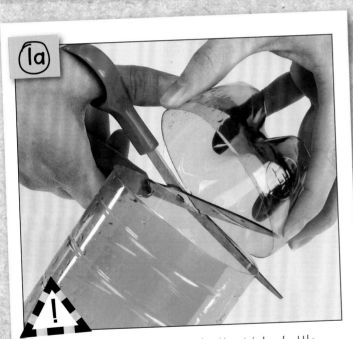

1a

Remove the cap of a large plastic drinks bottle. Using scissors, carefully cut off the bottom of the bottle.

1b

If the bottle gets wet with saliva, dry it

Blow up the balloon to the size of a ping-pong ball. Turn the top of the bottle upside down and drop the balloon into it. By blowing up into the bottle neck, try to blow the balloon out of the bottle.

Q Can you blow the balloon out?

A No, no matter how hard you blow! When you start blowing, the balloon is pushed up, but then the air from your lungs begins to flow under the balloon and around its sides. High-speed air has lower pressure than still air (this is called Bernoulli's principle). The pressure under the balloon falls, and the higher pressure air above the balloon pushes it down.

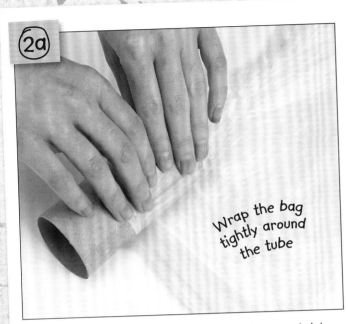

2a

Wrap the bag tightly around the tube

Place a card tube into the opening of a sandwich bag and wrap the bag's neck around it (so that the tube is the only passage into the bag).

2b

Try inflating the bag by putting your mouth against the end of the tube and blowing hard. Watch how the bag inflates.

2c

Now hold your mouth 10–20 cm away from the tube. Blow hard to make a narrow stream of air.

Q Which bag inflates faster?

A When you blow from far away the bag inflates faster. The fast-moving stream of air creates low pressure. This draws air in from around the entrance to the tube, which also goes into the bag, and it inflates faster.

Streamlined for SPEED

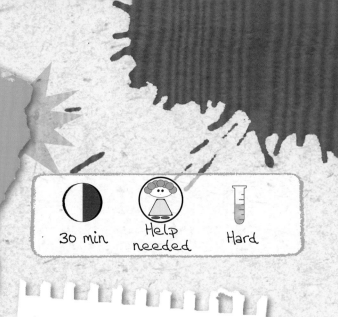

When you run, air pushes against you. This is called air resistance or drag. Air resistance pushes on anything that moves through the air. This experiment shows how.

30 min | Help needed | Hard

You will need

- work surface
- 3 strips of thin card, 8 cm by 25 cm
- 3 squares of thick card, 10 cm by 10 cm
- sticky tape
- stapler
- hair dryer

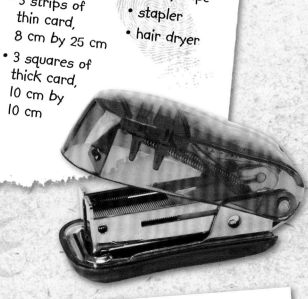

(a)

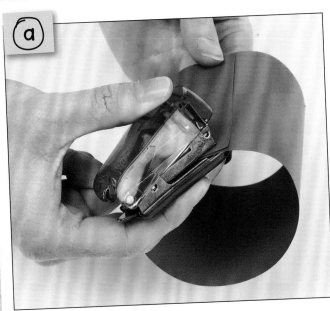

Roll one of the strips of card into a tube shape. Secure with a staple at each end.

(b)

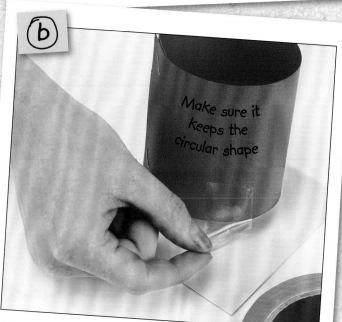

Make sure it keeps the circular shape

Attach the tube to the centre of a square of thick card with two pieces of sticky tape, one on each side.

(c)

Fold another strip of card into four equal pieces.

Stick the edges together with tape. Then fix the shape to a square of card with sticky tape.

The hair dryer should be level with your shapes

Stand the three tubes in line on a smooth table. Switch on a hair dryer and hold it about one metre away from the first shape. Slowly move the hair dryer towards the shape. At some point, the tube will begin to slide away. Try the same thing with the other two tubes.

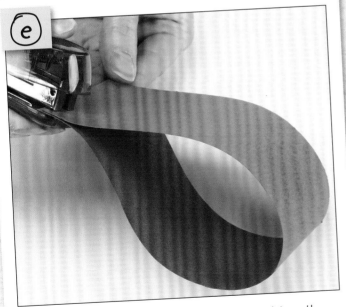

Press the ends of the third strip of card together to form a teardrop shape. Staple the ends of the card together and fix the shape to a square of card with sticky tape.

Q Which tube moves first?

A **The square tube moves first and the teardrop tube moves last.** Air flowing from the hair dryer hits the shapes, creating drag. The closer you move the hair dryer to the shapes, the faster air flows around them. And the faster the air flows, the greater the drag gets. Eventually drag becomes so great that it pushes the objects. The force of drag on an object depends on how easily air can flow around the object. The square creates the most drag and the teardrop the least. The teardrop is streamlined, allowing the air to flow smoothly around it.

FIRE extinguisher

Did you know that things cannot burn without air? But what happens to air when something does burn? Time to find out!

You will need

- work surface
- jug
- water
- matches
- small candle
- plate
- small, clean, empty jar
- large, clean, empty jar
- 3 coins, the same size
- modelling clay or sticky tack
- optional: food colouring

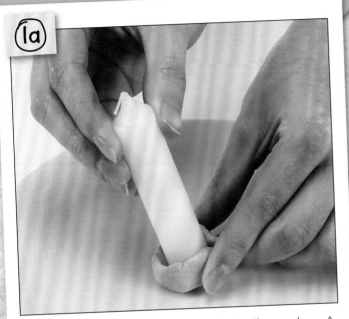

1a Put a small lump of modelling clay in the centre of a plate. Stick a candle into the clay so that it stands upright.

1b The jar should be taller than the candle

Light the candle and place the small jar over it. Count how many seconds it takes for the flame to go out.

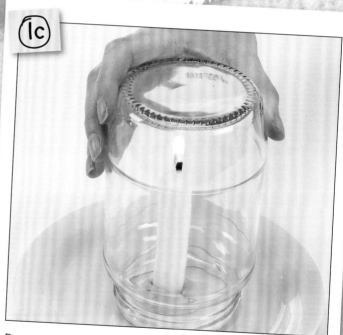

1c Repeat the experiment again with a large jar. Does the candle burn longer this time?

Which burns better?

A larger jar contains more air and so more oxygen, so the candle burns for longer. Air is a mixture of many different gases, but it is mostly nitrogen and oxygen. Oxygen is needed for burning. When you place the jar over a lit candle, the flame uses up oxygen. When the level of oxygen in the jar gets too low, the flame goes out.

2a

Make sure there's equal space between each coin

Put three coins around the candle. They will support the rim of the jar.

2c

Light the candle and put the jar over it, so that it rests on the coins.

2b

Pour coloured water (so you can see what's happening) onto the plate until it covers the coins.

Q What happens to the water?

A The water level rises as the candle goes out. This isn't caused by the oxygen being used up, but by the air in the jar cooling and contracting when the flame goes out.

Model DIVER

In this experiment you use both water pressure and air pressure to make a model dive and surface.

30 min   No help needed   Tricky

You will need

- work surface
- bendy straw
- paper clips
- large plastic drinks bottle with a lid
- glass
- scissors
- optional: food colouring

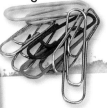

Preparation

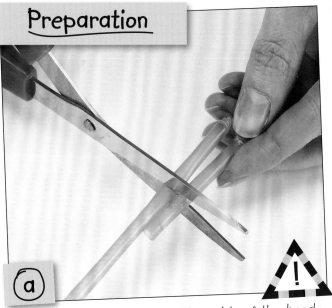

(a)

Cut the straw about 2 cm either side of the bendy section.

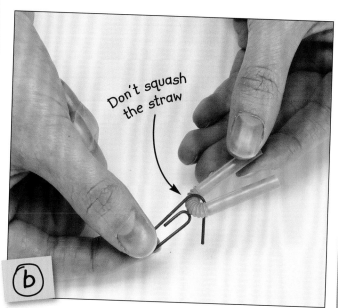

Don't squash the straw

(b)

Pull the ends of the straw to extend the bendy section. Unbend the outer loop of a paper clip and wrap it around the straw bend. This is your model diver.

Test your diver

(a)

Fill a glass with water to use as a testing tank. One at a time, add a paper clip to the bottom of the diver. Each time you add a clip, put the diver in the glass until it sinks.

When the diver finally sinks, remove one clip.

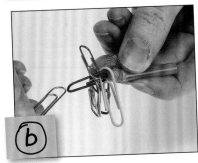

(b)

The model diver should then float.

(c)

30

1a

Fill a large plastic drinks bottle with water. Add food colouring for fun. Drop in your model diver and screw the lid onto the bottle.

Sinking...

sinking...

sunk!

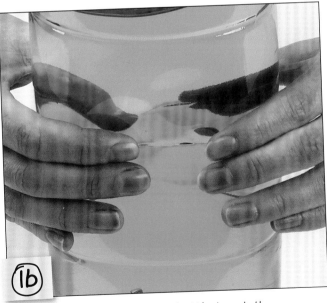

1b

Squeeze the middle of the bottle hard, then release your grip. If the diver does not dive and surface properly, remove it from the bottle and add or remove a paper clip.

Q **What happens to the diver?**

A **It sinks.** The straw is full of air and paper clips are needed to make it heavy enough to sink. When you squeeze the bottle, the air in the top of the bottle is squeezed into a smaller space. This increases the air pressure, which also increases the pressure inside the water. Water is squeezed into the straw, making it heavier, so the diver sinks. When the pressure is released, the air expands again. The water in the straw is forced out, making the diver lighter, and the straw surfaces.

RECORD
your results

You can record your test results here. Note down how successful the experiments were and what you have learnt about science from them. You could also write about how much you enjoyed each activity.

Add a picture of yourself as a scientist!

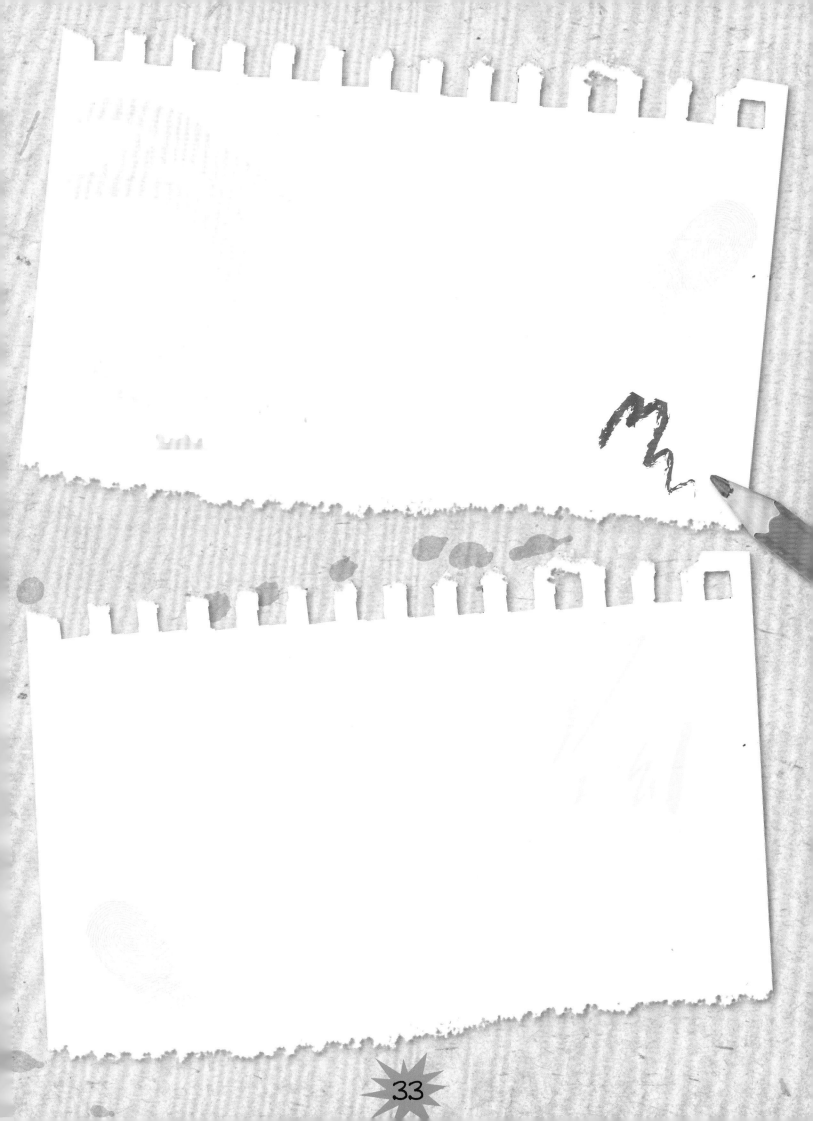

Quiz ZONE

Get ready to test how much you've learnt from the experiments in this book. Write down your answers on a piece of paper and then check them against the answers on page 40. No cheating!

Q5 picture clue

What are the missing words?

1. If the buoyant force on an object is less than its weight it will ... .

2. When water molecules at the surface are pulled towards each other it creates ... .

3. Bernoulli's principle states that high-speed air has ... pressure than still air.

4. Air resistance is also known as ... .

5. Things cannot burn without ... .

What word beginning with...

6. B happens when a jar of water is filled to the brim, but surface tension stops it from overflowing?

7. R means you use materials again in their original form rather than throwing them away?

Q6 picture clue

8. S describes an object that allows air to flow smoothly around it?

9. A is the blanket of air our planet is surrounded by?

True or false?

(10) An inflated balloon will sink.

(11) The higher up you go, the lower the air pressure.

(12) A fast-moving stream of air creates low pressure.

Q10 picture clue

Multiple choice

(13) In which of the following states can water exist at normal temperatures? A solid, a liquid, a gas, or all three?

(14) If two different-sized balloons are blown up and released at the same time, will the bigger balloon travel further, not so far or the same distance as the smaller balloon?

(15) Which direction does air pressure push? Up, down or in all directions?

(16) When air pushes against you, what is it called? Air pressure, surface tension or air resistance?

Remember, remember

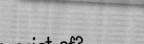

Q17 picture clue

(17) Does air weigh anything?

(18) Which two gases does air mainly consist of?

(19) At what temperature does water boil?

(20) What pushes water?

37

More questions this way

PICTURE Quiz

21 Which shape is the most streamlined?

22 Who will blow up the bag quicker?

23 Which of the following objects is most likely to sink in water?

24 In which jar will the candle burn for the longest time?

25 Which fountain has a higher water pressure?

38

GLOSSARY

Air A mixture of gases (mainly nitrogen and oxygen), dust and moisture.

Air pressure The force exerted by the weight of tiny particles of air.

Air resistance The push of air against a moving object.

Atmosphere A blanket of gases surrounding a planet, such as Earth, or a moon.

Bernoulli's principle The theory that high-speed air has lower pressure than still air.

Boiling point The temperature at which a liquid bubbles and changes into gas when it is heated.

Buoyancy When an object is able to float.

Drag Also known as air resistance.

Evaporation The process by which molecules change from liquid to gas when heated.

Expanding To become or make larger.

Floating An object will float on water if the upthrust is equal to or greater than the object's weight.

Inflate To fill a balloon, or other expandable object, with air or gas so that it becomes bigger.

Light A form of energy that we can see with our eyes.

Melting The process that changes a solid into a liquid, mainly when heated.

Nitrogen The gas that makes up the majority of air (78 percent).

Oxygen An essential gas to all living things. It makes up 21 percent of air.

Recycling When materials are taken to a plant where they can be melted and re-made into either the same or new products.

Re-using Using materials again in their original form rather than throwing them away.

Sinking An object will sink if its weight is greater than the upthrust of the water.

Streamlined An object that is shaped to move smoothly and easily, with little resistance, through air or water.

Surface tension Water molecules at the surface are pulled towards each other, and so act like a skin.

Upthrust The upward force a liquid pushes on a solid.

Water pressure The push of water caused by its weight. The deeper the water, the higher the pressure.

INDEX

QUIZ answers

1. Sink 2. Surface tension 3. Lower 4. Drag 5. Oxygen 6. Bulge 7. Re-using 8. Streamlined 9. Atmosphere 10. False 11. True 12. True 13. All three 14. Further 15. In all directions 16. Air resistance 17. Yes 18. Nitrogen and oxygen 19. 100°C 20. Water pressure 21. a 22. a 23. b 24. b 25. b